Scrumptious

SALMON
RECIPES

Salmon Recipes Made Easy For Beginners

Les Ilagan

DISCLAIMER

Content Arcade Publishing and its authors are joined together in their efforts to create these pages and their publications. Content Arcade Publishing and its authors make no assurance of any kind, stated or implied, with respect to the information provided.

LIMITS OF LIABILITY

Content Arcade Publishing and its authors shall not be held legally responsible in the event of incidental or consequential damages in line with or arising out of, the supplying of the information presented here.

Table of Contents

INTRODUCTION

This book offers a great selection of salmon recipes from the most basic to the ones that are exceptionally rich in flavor.

Salmon is one of the most favored alternatives to red meat and other meat products because of its versatility. Salmon is economically priced and available year-round, which makes it a great item to include in your weekly menu planning.

Cooking with salmon as the main ingredient is very easy and requires only a few minutes to cook. Just add some spices and herbs to enhance the flavor, you can have it grilled, baked, poached, broiled, or roasted. Either way, you can be sure that you will have a delicious dish on your table. Another good thing is that salmon goes very well in sandwiches, salads, and pasta dishes as well.

This book offers a wide selection of salmon recipes that will surely make your tummy happy!

Best Ways to Cook the Perfect Salmon

1.   It is best to leave the skin on when grilling your salmon. Start cooking with the skin-side down.
2.   When the recipe calls for boneless salmon fillets, remove pin bones carefully to keep the flesh intact.
3.   Enhance the flavor of your poached salmon by adding some garlic, lemon, spices, or herbs.
4.   Marinating your salmon before grilling, baking, or roasting will also give you a succulent dish.
5.   Before cooking your salmon, make sure to preheat the grill or oven.
6.   Leftover salmon can be recycled in making delicious salads, sandwiches, and pasta dishes.
7.   Salmon is done when you can easily flake the fillets with a fork, and the meat is opaque in color. Do not overcook your salmon, remove from heat once tested done. Overcooking it will only result in dry and undesirable salmon.
8.   You can turn the salmon once during cooking to have an even browning, and it is usually done halfway through.
9.   Never use tongs when turning your salmon, it is advisable to use a fish spatula instead. Salmon can easily break apart if handled with tongs during the cooking process.
10.   Thaw your frozen salmon inside the refrigerator; do not speed up the process by using the microwave oven or soak in hot water. It will lose its natural flavor and texture.

LUNCH & DINNER
RECIPES

EASY SALMON FRITTERS

Preparation Time	Total Time	Yield
10 minutes	25 minutes	8 servings

INGREDIENTS

- 16 ounces (450 g) canned salmon, drained
- 4 whole eggs (about 60 g each), beaten
- 1/2 cup (60 g) all-purpose flour
- 2 tablespoons (30 ml) olive oil
- 4 green onions (about 15 g), chopped
- Salt and freshly ground black pepper

METHOD

- Mix together the egg, onion, salmon, and flour in a large bowl. Season to taste.
- Put oil in a frying pan and place over medium-high flame. Spoon ¼ cup of salmon mixture into the pan, and by using the spatula, slightly press the patty to form round fritter. Cook for about 3-5 minutes on each side or until cooked through and golden brown.
- Transfer to a clean plate lined with paper towels. Repeat procedure for the remaining salmon mixture to make 8 fritters.
- Serve the fritters with steamed rice and veggies on the side, if desired.
- Enjoy.

NUTRITIONAL INFORMATION

Energy	Fat	Carbohydrates	Protein	Sodium
219 calories	121 g	13.2 g	15.2 g	217 mg

SALMON MUSHROOM AND DILL QUICHE

Preparation Time	Total Time	Yield
10 minutes	25 minutes	8 servings

INGREDIENTS

- 1 baked pie crust
- 2 tablespoons (30 ml) olive oil
- 2 shallots (about 40 g each), thinly sliced
- 2 teaspoons (6 g) garlic, minced
- 8 ounces (250 g) baked salmon, flaked
- 1 cup (150 g) button mushrooms, thinly sliced
- 2 tablespoons (7 g) chopped dill
- 3 large eggs (about 60 g each)
- 6 ounces (180 g) crumbled feta cheese
- Salt and freshly ground black pepper

METHOD

- Preheat and set your oven to 400 F (200 C).
- Put your pie crust in the pie pan or round baking dish.
- Heat the olive oil in a skillet over medium-high flame, stir-fry shallots and garlic for 2 minutes.
- Add the salmon, mushroom, and dill; cook for 5 minutes, stirring often. Then transfer the mixture onto the pie crust.
- Beat the eggs and stir in the feta cheese. Season to taste, and then pour over salmon mixture.
- Bake the quiche for 35-40 minutes or until completely set. Cool slightly before slicing.

- Serve and enjoy.

NUTRITIONAL INFORMATION

Energy	Fat	Carbohydrates	Protein	Sodium
265 calories	17.8 g	13.2 g	13.9 g	410 mg

SALMON BROCCOLI AND FETA QUICHE

Preparation Time	Total Time	Yield
10 minutes	25 minutes	8 servings

INGREDIENTS

- 1 pastry dough (about 1 lb. or 450 g)
- 2 cups (240 g) broccoli florets
- 6 ounces (180 g) canned salmon, drained
- 3/4 cup (45 g) spring onion
- 1 cup (150 g) feta cheese, diced
- 5 large eggs (about 60 g each)
- 3/4 cup (185 g) sour cream
- 1 ½ tablespoons (10 g) flour
- 1 tablespoon (15 g) mustard
- 1 tablespoon (3.5 g) chopped dill
- 1/2 teaspoon (2.5 g) salt
- 1/4 teaspoon (0.5 g) nutmeg

METHOD

- Start off by preheating oven to 400 F (200 C).
- Cover the base and sides of your deep dish pie plate with the pastry dough. Put pie weights on top of the dough and bake for 15 minutes. Set aside after removing the pie weights.
- Take your pie crust and put the broccoli, salmon, spring onion and feta.
- Whisk together the eggs, milk, mustard, sour cream, flour, dill, salt, and nutmeg. Pour this mixture over the

broccoli mixture in the crust.

- Put the quiche in the oven and bake for 50 minutes to an hour. Allow to cool down for 10 minutes before slicing.
- Serve and enjoy.

NUTRITIONAL INFORMATION

Energy	Fat	Carbohydrates	Protein	Sodium
258 calories	17.2 g	13.5 g	13.2 g	456 mg

SALMON AND CHERRY TOMATO QUICHE

Preparation Time	Total Time	Yield
15 minutes	15 minutes	4 servings

INGREDIENTS

- 2 tablespoons (30 ml) olive oil
- 1 medium (110 g) red onion, chopped
- 2 teaspoons (6 g) garlic, minced
- 1 cup (150 g) cherry tomatoes, halved
- 8 ounces (250 g) leftover baked salmon, cut into thin strips
- 1 tablespoon (3.5 g) dill weed, chopped
- 1 (9-inch) pie crust, unbaked
- 1/4 cup (30 g) cheddar cheese, grated
- 2 tablespoons (15 g) parmesan, grated
- 6 large eggs (about 60 g each)
- 2/3 cup (165 ml) milk
- 1/2 teaspoon (1 g) ground lemon pepper

METHOD

- Preheat and set your oven to 350 F (175 C).
- Heat oil in a large saucepan, add onion and garlic; stir-fry for about 3 minutes or until it becomes fragrant.
- Add the cherry tomatoes; cook, stirring occasionally until they are soft.
- Next, add the salmon and dill; cook for another 3-4 minutes. Remove from heat.
- Transfer the vegetable-salmon mixture into the pie

crust. Sprinkle with cheddar and parmesan.
- Whisk together the eggs and milk in a medium bowl. Then season with lemon pepper to taste. Pour the egg mixture over salmon mixture.
- Bake the quiche in the preheated oven for 30 to 40 minutes or until set. Cool slightly before serving.
- Enjoy.

NUTRITIONAL INFORMATION

Energy	Fat	Carbohydrates	Protein	Sodium
260 calories	16.6 g	11.8 g	16.5 g	232 mg

SMOKED SALMON OMELET WITH HERBS

Preparation Time	Total Time	Yield
5 minutes	10 minutes	4 servings

INGREDIENTS

- 4 ounces (125 g) smoked salmon, sliced thinly
- 6 whole eggs (about 60 g each)
- 1/2 cup (125 g) whole milk
- 1 tablespoon (3.5 g) dill, chopped
- 1 tablespoon (3.5 g) fresh parsley, chopped
- 1 tablespoon (15 g) butter
- Salt and freshly ground black pepper

METHOD

- Whisk the eggs along with the milk, salt, and pepper in a mixing bowl. Set aside.
- In a large non-stick frying pan, melt butter over a medium-low flame. Add the egg mixture and top with salmon, and then sprinkle with dill and parsley. Cover and cook for about 3 minutes or until cooked to your liking.
- Serve and enjoy.

NUTRITIONAL INFORMATION

Energy	Fat	Carbohydrates	Protein	Sodium
199 calories	14.6 g	2.3 g	14.7 g	515 mg

SALMON AND TOMATO OMELETTE WITH PARSLEY

Preparation Time	Total Time	Yield
5 minutes	10 minutes	4 servings

INGREDIENTS

- 4 large eggs (about 60 g each)
- 3 egg whites (about 40 g each)
- 2 tablespoons (30 ml) olive oil
- 1 shallot (about 40 g), thinly sliced
- 1 teaspoon (3 g) garlic, crushed
- 1 cup (150 g) cherry tomatoes, halved
- 2 ounces (60 g) smoked salmon, chopped
- 2 tablespoons (7 g) fresh parsley, chopped
- Salt and freshly ground black pepper

METHOD

- In a mixing bowl, beat the eggs, and then season with salt and pepper.
- Heat 1 tablespoon olive oil in a non-stick pan, stir-fry shallot and garlic for 2-3 minutes.
- Add the cherry tomatoes and salmon; cook for 3-4 minutes. Transfer to a clean plate and then set aside.
- Heat the remaining oil using the same pan. Pour the egg and cook for about 2 minutes. Gently lift the edge of the egg mixture with a spatula, let the uncooked egg mixture flow to the edges of the pan to cook.

- Top half of the egg with tomato-salmon mixture. Then sprinkle with parsley. Gently lift the other side to cover the filling; cook for 2 minutes more.
- Transfer to a serving dish.
- Serve and enjoy.

NUTRITIONAL INFORMATION

Energy	Fat	Carbohydrates	Protein	Sodium
173 calories	12.2 g	5.2 g	11.6 g	305 mg

SALMON AND ZUCCHINI RISOTTO

Preparation Time	Total Time	Yield
10 minutes	35 minutes	6 servings

INGREDIENTS

- 3 cups (750 ml) vegetable stock
- 2 cups (500 ml) water
- 2 tablespoons (30 ml) olive oil
- 1/2 cup (30 g) scallions, chopped
- 1 tablespoon (10 g) garlic, minced
- 1 ½ cups (280 g) Arborio rice
- 1/2 cup (125 ml) dry white wine
- 1 medium (200 g) zucchini, diced
- 8 ounces (250 g) baked salmon fillet, flaked
- 2/3 cup (165 g) half and half cream
- 1 tablespoon (3.5 g) fresh thyme, chopped
- 1/2 teaspoon (1 g) ground coriander seeds
- Salt and freshly ground black pepper

METHOD

- Bring the vegetable stock and water to a boil in a stockpot over medium flame.
- In a heavy-bottomed saucepan, stir-fry scallions and garlic in oil until fragrant.
- Add the rice and stir until well coated with oil; cook for 2 minutes.
- Add the wine; cook, stirring until absorbed.
- Add the zucchini and vegetable stock one ladleful at a

time, stirring often. Cook the rice for about 20 minutes or until al dente.

- Add the salmon, cream, thyme, and coriander towards the last 5-7 minutes of cooking time. Season to taste.
- Transfer to a serving dish.
- Serve immediately and enjoy.

NUTRITIONAL INFORMATION

Energy	Fat	Carbohydrates	Protein	Sodium
349 calories	12.4 g	42.4 g	13.6 g	148 mg

RISOTTO WITH SALMON AND PEAS

Preparation Time	Total Time	Yield
15 minutes	30 minutes	6 servings

INGREDIENTS

- 2 cups (500 ml) clam juice
- 1 cup (250 ml) water
- 2 tablespoons (30 g) unsalted butter
- 2 shallots (about 40 g each), chopped
- 2 teaspoons (6 g) garlic, minced
- 1 cup (185 g) Arborio rice
- 1/3 cup (85 ml) dry white wine
- 8 ounces (250 g) baked salmon fillet, diced
- 1/2 cup (85 g) frozen green peas, thawed
- 2/3 cup (165 ml) milk
- 2 tablespoons (7 g) fresh parsley, chopped
- Salt and freshly ground black pepper

METHOD

- Bring the clam juice and water to a boil in a stockpot over medium flame. Remove from heat.
- In a heavy-bottomed saucepan, stir-fry shallots and garlic in butter over medium heat until fragrant.
- Add the rice and stir until well coated with oil; cook for 2 minutes.
- Add the wine; cook, stirring often until absorbed.
- Add the clam juice one ladleful at a time, stirring often. Cook the rice for about 20 minutes or until al dente.

- Add the salmon, peas, milk, and parsley towards the last 5–7 minutes of cooking time. Season to taste.
- Transfer to a serving dish.
- Serve immediately and enjoy.

NUTRITIONAL INFORMATION

Energy	Fat	Carbohydrates	Protein	Sodium
309 calories	8.2 g	40.8 g	14.8 g	267 mg

PAN-FRIED SALMON WITH POTATOES AND HERBS

Preparation Time	Total Time	Yield
15 minutes	30 minutes	4 servings

INGREDIENTS

- 4 (5 oz. or 150 g) salmon fillet with skin
- 2 tablespoons (30 ml) olive oil
- 1 tablespoon (3.5 g) dill weed, chopped
- Salt and freshly ground black pepper
- Baked marble potatoes, to serve
- Fresh salad greens, to serve

METHOD

- Brush salmon with oil and season to taste. Then, sprinkle with dill.
- Heat a large non-stick frying pan over medium flame, put the salmon skin side down and cook for 4-5 minutes or until skin is brown and crisp. Turn the salmon and cook for another 2-3 minutes or until cooked through.
- Serve with baked marble potatoes and fresh salad greens on the side.
- Enjoy..

NUTRITIONAL INFORMATION

Energy	Fat	Carbohydrates	Protein	Sodium
172 calories	9.0 g	0.4 g	23.2 g	219 mg

BAKED SALMON WITH PESTO SAUCE

Preparation Time	Total Time	Yield
15 minutes	30 minutes	4 servings

INGREDIENTS

- 4 (5 oz. or 150 g) fresh salmon steaks
- 1/4 cup (60 g) homemade basil pesto sauce
- 1 tablespoon (15 ml) olive oil
- 1 tablespoon (10 g) lemon zest, finely grated
- Salt and freshly ground black pepper
- Garden fresh salad, to serve

METHOD

- Preheat and set your oven to 420 F (210 C).
- In a small bowl, whisk together the pesto, olive oil, and lemon zest.
- Arrange the salmon fillets in a baking dish and season to taste. Spoon pesto mixture over salmon and spread evenly.
- Bake the salmon for about 12-15 minutes or until cooked through.
- Serve with garden salad and enjoy.

NUTRITIONAL INFORMATION

Energy	Fat	Carbohydrates	Protein	Sodium
249 calories	16.9 g	1.3 g	23.5 g	292 mg

CUMIN-SPICED BAKED SALMON WITH TARTAR SAUCE

Preparation Time	Total Time	Yield
15 minutes	30 minutes	4 servings

INGREDIENTS

- 2 tablespoons (30 ml) olive oil
- 1 tablespoon (10 g) lemon zest, finely grated
- 1/2 teaspoon (1 g) cumin, ground
- 1/2 teaspoon (1 g) garlic powder
- 4 (5 oz. or 150 g) fresh salmon fillets
- Salt and freshly ground black pepper

Tartar Sauce:

- 1/4 cup (60 g) low-fat mayonnaise
- 2 tablespoons (30 ml) fresh lemon juice
- 1 teaspoon (5 g) pickle relish
- 1 shallot (about 40 g), minced
- 1 (3 g) clove garlic minced

METHOD

- Preheat your oven to 420 F (210 C).
- In a small bowl, whisk together mayonnaise, lemon juice, pickle relish, shallot, and garlic. Cover and keep refrigerated until ready to serve.
- Combine olive oil, lemon zest, cumin, and garlic powder in a shallow baking dish. Add the salmon fillets and rub the spice mixture on all sides.

- Arrange the salmon fillets in a baking dish and season to taste.
- Bake for about 12-15 minutes or until cooked through.
- Serve with prepared tartar sauce.
- Enjoy.

NUTRITIONAL INFORMATION

Energy	Fat	Carbohydrates	Protein	Sodium
249 calories	15.7 g	5.1 g	22.6 g	351 mg

GRILLED SALMON WITH GARLIC LEMON AND SAGE

Preparation Time	Total Time	Yield
15 minutes	30 minutes	4 servings

INGREDIENTS

- 4 (5 oz. or 150 g) salmon fillets
- 2 tablespoons (30 ml) extra-virgin olive oil
- 2 tablespoons (30 ml) lemon juice
- 1 teaspoon (3 g) garlic, crushed
- 1 teaspoon (2 g) fresh sage, minced
- 1/2 teaspoon (2.5 g) kosher salt
- 1/4 teaspoon (0.5 g) ground black pepper
- 1 teaspoon (3 g) lemon zest, finely grated
- Lemon wedges, to serve

METHOD

- Heat up the grill on high.
- Meanwhile, whisk together the oil, lemon juice, garlic, sage, salt, pepper, and lemon zest; rub this mixture all over fillets.
- Grill the salmon for 3-4 minutes on each side, or until just cooked.
- Transfer to a serving dish and garnish with lemon wedges.
- Serve and enjoy.

NUTRITIONAL INFORMATION

Energy	Fat	Carbohydrates	Protein	Sodium
213 calories	14.1 g	0.4 g	22.1 g	342 mg

SPICED ROASTED SALMON AND VEGGIES

Preparation Time	Total Time	Yield
15 minutes	30 minutes	4 servings

INGREDIENTS

- 1/2 teaspoon (1 g) cumin, ground
- 1/2 teaspoon (1 g) coriander, ground
- 1/2 teaspoon (1 g) sweet paprika
- 1/4 teaspoon (0.5 g) allspice, ground
- 1/4 teaspoon (1.5 g) salt
- 1/4 teaspoon (0.5 g) ground black pepper
- 4 (5 oz. or 150 g) salmon fillets
- 2 tablespoons (30 ml) olive oil
- 2 tablespoons (30 ml) lemon juice
- 1 tablespoon (3.5 g) fresh rosemary, chopped
- 4 medium boiled potatoes (about 200 g each), quartered
- 1/2 pound (225 g) green beans, trimmed

METHOD

- Preheat and set your oven to 450 F (225 C).
- Combine the salt, cumin, coriander seed, paprika, all spice, and pepper in a shallow dish. Rub salmon with this mixture until coated well. Set aside.
- In a small bowl, mix together oil, lemon juice, and rosemary.
- Place the green beans and potatoes in a baking dish. Brush with olive oil mixture. Top with salmon and brush with remaining olive oil mixture.

- Bake in the oven for 10-15 minutes or until salmon is cooked through.
- Serve and enjoy.

NUTRITIONAL INFORMATION

Energy	Fat	Carbohydrates	Protein	Sodium
311 calories	12 g	39 g	26 g	216 mg

ROASTED SALMON AND ASPARAGUS WITH PESTO

Preparation Time	Total Time	Yield
15 minutes	30 minutes	4 servings

INGREDIENTS

- 4 (5 oz. or 150 g) fresh salmon steak
- 1/4 cup (60 g) basil pesto sauce
- 1 tablespoon (15 ml) olive oil
- 1 tablespoon (15 ml) lime zest, finely grated
- 8 ounces (250 g) fresh asparagus, trimmed
- Salt and freshly ground black pepper

METHOD

- Preheat and set your oven at 400 F (200 C).
- In a small bowl, combine the pesto, lime zest, and olive oil.
- Arrange the asparagus in a baking dish, and then top with salmon and season to taste. Spoon pesto mixture over salmon and spread evenly.
- Bake in the preheated oven for about 12–15 minutes or until cooked through.
- Serve and enjoy.

NUTRITIONAL INFORMATION

Energy	Fat	Carbohydrates	Protein	Sodium
286 calories	19.6 g	3.2 g	25.7 g	219 mg

GRILLED CAJUN SALMON

Preparation Time	Total Time	Yield
15 minutes	30 minutes	4 servings

INGREDIENTS

- 4 (5 oz. or 150 g) salmon fillet, with skin
- 1 tablespoon (15 g) butter, melted
- 1 teaspoon (2 g) onion powder
- 1/2 teaspoon (1 g) dried thyme
- 1/2 teaspoon (1 g) cayenne pepper
- 1/2 teaspoon (1 g) cumin, ground
- 1/2 teaspoon (1 g) coriander seed, ground
- 1/4 teaspoon (1.5 g) sea salt
- 1/4 teaspoon (0.5 g) freshly ground black pepper
- Lemon wedges, to serve
- Tossed greens, to serve

METHOD

- Mix onion powder, dried thyme, cayenne pepper, cumin, coriander, salt, and pepper in a small bowl.
- Brush salmon with melted butter then rub with spice mixture, covering all sides.
- Heat your grill or griddle over medium-high and cook the salmon for about 3-4 minutes on each side or to your desired doneness.
- Serve with lemon wedges and some tossed greens on the side.

NUTRITIONAL INFORMATION

Energy	Fat	Carbohydrates	Protein	Sodium
245 calories	14.6 g	1.4 g	27.8 g	222 mg

GLAZED SALMON IN SWEET CHILI AND LIME

Preparation Time	Total Time	Yield
15 minutes	25 minutes	4 servings

INGREDIENTS

- 4 (5 oz. or 150 g) salmon fillet, boneless
- 2 tablespoons (30 ml) soy sauce
- 2 tablespoons (30 ml) lime juice
- 1 tablespoon (10 g) lime zest
- 1/4 cup (60 g) sweet-chili sauce

METHOD

- Preheat your grill to high.
- Whisk together the lime juice, zest, soy sauce, and sweet chili sauce in a small glass bowl. Reserve half of the mixture. Add the salmon in the mixture and coat all sides evenly.
- Grill salmon for 5 minutes on each side or until cooked through. Brushing with reserved sauce occasionally.
- Serve and enjoy.

NUTRITIONAL INFORMATION

Energy	Fat	Carbohydrates	Protein	Sodium
241 calories	8.8 g	12.8 g	27.8 g	498 mg

SPICY SALMON WITH HONEY-GINGER GLAZE

Preparation Time	Total Time	Yield
10 minutes	20 minutes	4 servings

INGREDIENTS

- 4 (5 oz. or 150 g) fresh salmon fillets
- 1 teaspoon (2 g) cayenne pepper
- 1/2 teaspoon (1 g) cumin, ground
- 2 tablespoons (30 g) butter
- 1 tablespoon (10 g) fresh ginger, finely grated
- 1/4 cup (25 ml) rice vinegar
- 2 tablespoons (40 ml) honey
- 1 tablespoon (15 ml) soy sauce
- Salt and freshly ground black pepper

METHOD

- Rub the salmon fillets with cumin and cayenne pepper. Season to taste.
- Heat butter in a non-stick frying pan over medium heat. Cook salmon for 3-4 minutes on each side or until golden and cooked through. Transfer to a clean plate and tent with foil to keep warm.
- Using the same pan, stir-fry ginger until it becomes fragrant. Add the vinegar, honey, and soy sauce; cook for 2-3 minutes more. Season with pepper to taste. Remove from heat.
- Drizzle honey-ginger glaze over the salmon on your serving dish.

- Serve and enjoy.

NUTRITIONAL INFORMATION

Energy	Fat	Carbohydrates	Protein	Sodium
288 calories	14.7 g	10.1 g	27.9 g	486 mg

SOY GARLIC BROILED SALMON

Preparation Time	Total Time	Yield
35 minutes	50 minutes	4 servings

INGREDIENTS

- 4 (5 oz. or 150 g) salmon fillets
- 2 tablespoons (30 ml) soybean oil
- 2 tablespoons (30 ml) soy sauce
- 2 tablespoons (30 ml) lemon juice
- 1/2 teaspoon (1 g) lemon pepper, ground
- 2 teaspoons (6 g) garlic, crushed
- 1 tablespoon (3.5 g) fresh rosemary, chopped
- Salt and freshly ground black pepper

METHOD

- Combine the oil, soy sauce, lemon juice, lemon pepper, garlic, and rosemary in a glass baking dish. Mix well.
- Add salmon fillets, flesh-side down. Cover and allow to marinate in the fridge for at least 30 minutes.
- Preheat your broiler to medium-high.
- Place the salmon in the broiler and cook for about 10-12 minutes or until golden.
- Serve and enjoy.

NUTRITIONAL INFORMATION

Energy	Fat	Carbohydrates	Protein	Sodium
260 calories	16.0 g	2.1 g	28.3 g	316 mg

SALMON KEBABS WITH LEMON AND ROSEMARY

Preparation Time	Total Time	Yield
15 minutes	25 minutes	4 servings

INGREDIENTS

- 1 lb. (450 g) salmon fillet, cubed
- 2 tablespoons (30 ml) olive oil
- 2 tablespoons (30 ml) lemon juice
- 1 tablespoon (10 g) lemon zest, finely grated
- 1 tablespoon (3.5 g) fresh rosemary, chopped
- Salt and freshly ground black pepper
- Wooden skewers

METHOD

- Preheat your grill to high.
- Whisk together oil, lemon juice, zest, and rosemary in a mixing bowl. Add the salmon and turn to coat all sides evenly. Season to taste.
- Thread salmon onto the skewers. Grill for about 3-4 minutes on each side or until just cooked.
- Serve and enjoy.

NUTRITIONAL INFORMATION

Energy	Fat	Carbohydrates	Protein	Sodium
223 calories	14.2 g	2.5 g	22.1 g	182 mg

ASIAN BAKED SALMON RECIPE

Preparation Time	Total Time	Yield
15 minutes	30 minutes	4 servings

INGREDIENTS

- 4 (5 oz. or 150 g) salmon fillet
- 2 tablespoons (30 ml) soy light sauce
- 1 tablespoon (15 ml) lemon juice
- 1 tablespoon (15 g) oyster sauce
- 1 tablespoon (15 g) hoisin sauce
- 1 tablespoon (10 g) fresh ginger, finely grated
- Steamed white rice, to serve
- Lemon slices, for garnish

METHOD

- Preheat and set your oven to 400 F (200 C).
- Combine the soy sauce, lemon juice, oyster sauce, hoisin sauce, and ginger in a small bowl.
- Place salmon in a shallow baking dish and pour the sauce over fish, cover with foil.
- Bake the salmon in the preheated oven for 10 minutes or until cooked through.
- Serve salmon on top of rice, drizzled with sauce from the baking dish. Garnish with lemon slices.
- Enjoy.

NUTRITIONAL INFORMATION

Energy	Fat	Carbohydrates	Protein	Sodium
188 calories	8.2 g	3.1 g	25.6 g	407 mg

GRILLED SALMON WITH HONEY MUSTARD SAUCE

Preparation Time	Total Time	Yield
15 minutes	25 minutes	4 servings

INGREDIENTS

- 4 (5 oz. or 150 g) salmon fillet
- 1 tablespoon (15 ml) olive oil
- Salt and freshly ground black pepper
- 2 tablespoons (30 g) unsalted butter
- 1 tablespoon (7 g) all-purpose flour
- 1/4 cup (60 ml) dry wine
- 2 tablespoons (30 ml) Dijon mustard
- 1 teaspoon (5 g) wholegrain mustard
- 2 tablespoons (30 ml) fresh lemon juice
- 1 teaspoon (3 g) garlic, crushed
- Mashed potatoes, to serve

METHOD

- Preheat your grill to high.
- Heat butter in a small saucepan. Stir in flour until dissolved. Add the Dijon mustard, wholegrain mustard, lemon juice, wine, and garlic. Cook for 3 minutes, stirring frequently. Remove from heat.
- Drizzle oil on salmon and season to taste.
- Grill salmon for 4-5 minutes on each side or until cooked through.

- Serve salmon on top of mashed potatoes. Drizzle with mustard sauce.

NUTRITIONAL INFORMATION

Energy	Fat	Carbohydrates	Protein	Sodium
294 calories	17.9 g	4.8 g	26.0 g	277 mg

GRILLED HONEY CITRUS SALMON

Preparation Time	Total Time	Yield
15 minutes	25 minutes	4 servings

INGREDIENTS

- 4 (5 oz. or 150 g) salmon fillet
- 1/2 cup (125 ml) fresh orange juice
- 2 tablespoons (30 ml) lemon juice
- 2 tablespoons (30 ml) olive oil
- 2 tablespoons (40 ml) honey
- Salt and freshly ground black pepper
- Lemon slices, for garnish

METHOD

- Preheat your grill to high.
- Whisk the oil, lemon juice, orange juice, and honey in a mixing bowl. Reserve half of the mixture.
- Add the salmon in the bowl and turn to coat all sides. Season to taste.
- Grill for 4-5 minutes on each side until cooked, brushing with reserved sauce occasionally.
- Transfer to a serving dish and garnish with lemon slices.
- Serve and enjoy.

NUTRITIONAL INFORMATION

Energy	Fat	Carbohydrates	Protein	Sodium
242 calories	11.5 g	11.0 g	25.0 g	206 mg

POACHED SALMON WITH LEMON

Preparation Time	Total Time	Yield
15 minutes	25 minutes	4 servings

INGREDIENTS

- 4 (5 oz. or 150 g) salmon fillet, skin on
- 1/2 cup (125 ml) dry white wine
- 1/4 cup (60 ml) lemon juice
- 1 tablespoon (10 g) lemon zest
- 2 bay leaves, dried
- 1/2 teaspoon (1 g) whole black peppercorns
- 2 cups (500 ml) water
- Lemon slices, for garnish
- Salt and pepper, to taste

METHOD

- Simmer the wine, lemon, lemon zest, bay leaves, peppercorn, and water in a large frying pan over medium flame.
- Add the salmon, cover and allow to cook for roughly 10 minutes. Remove salmon using a slotted spoon. Season to taste.
- Serve and enjoy.

NUTRITIONAL INFORMATION

Energy	Fat	Carbohydrates	Protein	Sodium
201 calories	8.1 g	2.0 g	25.0 g	215 mg

SALMON AND COTTAGE CHEESE PATTIES WITH CHIVES

Preparation Time	Total Time	Yield
15 minutes	30 minutes	4 servings

INGREDIENTS

- 16 oz. (450 g) canned salmon, flaked
- 1/2 cup (125 g) mashed potatoes
- 1/2 cup (110 g) cottage cheese
- 1/2 cup (50 g) breadcrumbs
- 1 shallot (about 40 g), chopped
- 1 (60 g) whole egg, lightly beaten
- 2 tablespoons (7 g) fresh coriander or cilantro, chopped
- 2 tablespoons (30 ml) olive oil
- Salt and freshly ground black pepper

METHOD

- Combine the salmon, mashed potatoes, cottage cheese, breadcrumbs, shallot, egg, and coriander in a mixing bowl. Season with salt and pepper. Mix well.
- Spoon about 2 Tbsp. mixture and form into small patties.
- Heat the oil in a non-stick frying pan, cook salmon patties for 3-4 minutes on each side or until brown.
- Serve and enjoy.

NUTRITIONAL INFORMATION

Energy	Fat	Carbohydrates	Protein	Sodium
188 calories	10.6 g	8.7 g	15.1 g	185 mg

SALMON AND VEGGIE BURGER PATTIES

Preparation Time	Total Time	Yield
15 minutes	30 minutes	6 servings

INGREDIENTS

- 12 oz. (340 g) canned pink salmon, drained and flaked
- 1 medium (60 g) carrot, finely chopped
- 1/2 cup (125 g) mashed potatoes
- 1/2 cup (50 g) breadcrumbs
- 1/4 cup (15 g) green onions, chopped
- 1 teaspoon (3 g) garlic, minced
- 1 large egg (about 60 g), lightly beaten
- 1 tablespoon (15 ml) Worcestershire sauce
- 2 tablespoons (30 ml) olive oil
- Salt and pepper, to taste

METHOD

- Combine salmon, carrot, green onions, garlic, mashed potatoes, breadcrumbs, Worcestershire sauce, and egg in a mixing bowl. Season with salt and pepper. Mix well.
- Divide the salmon mixture to form 6 patties.
- Heat oil in a non-stick frying pan. Cook salmon patties for about 3-4 minutes on each side or until brown.
- Serve and enjoy.

NUTRITIONAL INFORMATION

Energy	Fat	Carbohydrates	Protein	Sodium
182 calories	10.8 g	8.3 g	13.7 g	213 mg

EASY GRILLED SALMON RECIPE

Preparation Time	Total Time	Yield
20 minutes	20 minutes	4 servings

INGREDIENTS

- 4 (5 oz. or 150 g) fresh salmon fillets
- 2 tablespoons (30 ml) olive oil
- 2 tablespoons (30 ml) lemon juice
- 1/2 teaspoon (1 g) garlic powder
- 1/2 teaspoon (1 g) lemon pepper

METHOD

- In a glass baking dish, mix together the oil, lemon juice, garlic powder, and lemon pepper. Place salmon flesh-side down. Cover and allow to marinate in the fridge for at least 30 minutes.
- Preheat your grill or griddle to medium-high.
- Grill the salmon fillets for 3-4 minutes on each side or until grill marks form and cooked through.
- Serve and enjoy.

NUTRITIONAL INFORMATION

Energy	Fat	Carbohydrates	Protein	Sodium
232 calories	14.8 g	0.6 g	24.9 g	24.9 mg

ASIAN-STYLED BAKED SALMON

Preparation Time	Total Time	Yield
10 minutes	55 minutes	4 servings

INGREDIENTS

- 2.2 lbs. (1 kg) skinless salmon fillet
- 1 tablespoon (15 g) lemon zest, grated
- 1/4 cup (15 g) fresh coriander, chopped
- 1/4 cup (60 ml) soy sauce
- 3 tablespoons (45 ml) lemon juice
- 1 teaspoon (3.5 g) fresh ginger, grated
- 4 (3 g) garlic cloves, minced
- 1/4 cup (80 ml) honey
- 1/4 cup fresh chives (about 15 g), finely chopped
- Salt and freshly ground black pepper

METHOD

- In a glass baking dish, mix together the lemon zest, lemon juice, soy sauce, coriander, ginger, and garlic. Put salmon in the mixture and coat all sides evenly. Cover and keep refrigerated for 20-30 minutes.
- Preheat and set your oven to 200 C or 400 F.
- Brush salmon with honey and bake for 10-12 minutes or until just cooked.
- Transfer salmon to a serving platter, sprinkle with fresh chives. Garnish with lemon slices, if desired.
- Serve and enjoy.

NUTRITIONAL INFORMATION

Energy	Fat	Carbohydrates	Protein	Sodium
198 calories	6.6 g	10.6 g	24.6 g	343 mg

GRILLED BALSAMIC SALMON WITH ROSEMARY

Preparation Time	Total Time	Yield
10 minutes	40 minutes	4 servings

INGREDIENTS

- 4 (5 oz. 150 g) salmon fillets
- 2 tablespoons (30 ml) balsamic vinegar
- 2 tablespoons (30 ml) olive oil
- 1 tablespoon (15 g) Dijon mustard
- 2 (3 g) cloves garlic, minced
- 1 sprig fresh rosemary, minced
- Salt and freshly ground black pepper

METHOD

- Whisk together the balsamic vinegar, olive oil, Dijon mustard, garlic, and rosemary in a shallow ceramic dish. Add the salmon fillets and turn to coat all sides. Cover and refrigerate for 30 minutes to absorb flavors.
- Grill the salmon fillets over medium-high heat for about 5 minutes on each side or until grill marks form and fish is cooked through.
- Transfer to a serving dish.
- Serve and enjoy.

NUTRITIONAL INFORMATION

Energy	Fat	Carbohydrates	Protein	Sodium
219 calories	14 g	1.0 g	22 g	243 mg

SPICED SALMON AND VEGGIE KEBABS

Preparation Time	Total Time	Yield
15 minutes	30 minutes	4 servings

INGREDIENTS

- 2.2 lbs. (1 kg) salmon fillet, cubed
- 2 medium onion (about 110 g each), quartered
- 1 medium (120 g) red bell pepper, cut into 1-inch pieces
- 1 medium (120 g) green bell pepper, cut into 1-inch pieces
- 1 cup (150 g) button mushrooms
- 1/4 cup (60 ml) olive oil
- 2 tablespoons (30 ml) lemon juice
- 1 teaspoon (2 g) cumin, ground
- 1 teaspoon (2 g) paprika
- Salt and freshly ground black pepper
- Wooden skewers

METHOD

- Preheat your grill to high.
- Whisk together the oil, lemon juice, cumin, and paprika in a mixing bowl. Season with salt and pepper. Reserve half of the mixture.
- Put the salmon in the bowl with mixture and coat all sides evenly.
- Thread the salmon alternately with vegetables onto the skewers.
- Grill for about 3-4 minutes on each side or until just cooked. Brushing with reserved oil mixture occasionally.

- Serve and enjoy.

NUTRITIONAL INFORMATION

Energy	Fat	Carbohydrates	Protein	Sodium
220 calories	12.5 g	5.5 g	23.1 g	201 mg

GRILLED SALMON WITH ORANGE GLAZE

Preparation Time	Total Time	Yield
15 minutes	35 minutes	4 servings

INGREDIENTS

- 4 (5 oz. or 150 g) salmon fillet, boneless
- 1/2 cup (125 ml) fresh orange juice
- 1 tablespoon (10 g) orange zest, finely grated
- 2 tablespoons (40 ml) honey
- 2 tablespoons (30 ml) olive oil
- Steamed snap peas, to serve
- Steamed brown rice, to serve

METHOD

- Preheat your grill to high.
- Whisk the orange juice, zest, honey, and oil in a small glass bowl. Reserve half of the mixture.
- Put the salmon in the bowl with orange mixture and coat all sides evenly. Season with salt and pepper. Cover and refrigerate for 30 minutes.
- Grill for about 4-5 minutes on each side or until just cooked. Brushing with reserved orange mixture, frequently.
- Serve with steamed snap peas and brown rice on the side.
- Enjoy.

NUTRITIONAL INFORMATION

Energy	Fat	Carbohydrates	Protein	Sodium
281 calories	13.8 g	15.5 g	25.3 g	198 mg

STEAMED SALMON WITH LEMON AND CHIVES

Preparation Time	Total Time	Yield
20 minutes	20 minutes	4 servings

INGREDIENTS

- 4 (5 oz. or 150 g) salmon fillet
- 2 tablespoons (30 ml) olive oil
- 2 tablespoons (30 ml) lemon juice
- 2 tablespoons (7 g) fresh chives, chopped
- Lemon wedges, to serve
- Salt and freshly ground black pepper

METHOD

- Mix together the oil, lemon juice, and chives in a small glass bowl. Season with salt and pepper. Set aside.
- Cut a sheet of aluminum foil to make a pocket just enough for 4 salmon fillets, fold upward all sides to prevent juice to spill. Put the salmon into the foil pocket and some lemon vinaigrette.
- Place steamer half-filled with water over medium-high flame and bring to a boil.
- Arrange the foil pocket with salmon into the steamer. Cover and cook for 8-10 minutes.
- Transfer salmon into a serving dish. Garnish with lemon wedges.
- Serve and enjoy.

NUTRITIONAL INFORMATION

Energy	Fat	Carbohydrates	Protein	Sodium
231 calories	14.9 g	0.2 g	24.9 g	205 mg

PAN-FRIED SALMON WITH MIXED VEGETABLES

Preparation Time	Total Time	Yield
15 minutes	25 minutes	4 servings

INGREDIENTS

- 4 (5 oz. or 150 g) salmon fillet
- 2 tablespoons (30 ml) olive oil
- 2 tablespoons (30 ml) lime juice
- 3 cups (360 g) broccoli florets, cut into small pieces
- 1 medium (60 g) carrot, diced
- 2 tablespoons (7 g) fresh parsley, finely chopped
- Lime wedges, to serve
- Salt and freshly ground black pepper

METHOD

- Brush the salmon with lime juice and then season with salt and pepper.
- Heat oil in a non-stick frying pan over medium-high flame. Cook the salmon for 3-4 minutes on each side or until golden. Transfer to a clean plate and cover to keep warm.
- Combine the broccoli florets and carrots in a steamer basket.
- Place the steamer half-filled with water over medium-high flame and bring to a boil. Put the steamer basket with vegetables into the steamer. Cover and allow to

cook for 7-8 minutes or until crisp-tender. Season with salt and pepper.

- Transfer the cooked vegetables into a serving dish. Top with salmon and sprinkle with parsley.
- Serve and enjoy.

NUTRITIONAL INFORMATION

Energy	Fat	Carbohydrates	Protein	Sodium
260 calories	15.1 g	2.2 g	26.9 g	238 mg

ROASTED SALMON AND VEGGIES

Preparation Time	Total Time	Yield
15 minutes	35 minutes	4 servings

INGREDIENTS

- 4 (5 oz. or 150 g) salmon fillet
- 2 tablespoons (30 ml) olive oil
- 2 tablespoons (30 ml) soy sauce
- 2 tablespoons (30 ml) balsamic vinegar
- 1 medium (200 g) zucchini, cut into pieces
- 2 medium tomatoes (about 125 g each), cut into small pieces
- 1 medium (120 g) green bell pepper, cut into small pieces
- Steamed white rice, to serve
- Lemon slices, for garnish
- Salt and pepper, to taste

METHOD

- Preheat and set your oven to 400 F (200 C).
- Whisk the oil, soy sauce, and balsamic vinegar in a small bowl.
- Place the vegetables in a shallow baking dish and top with salmon. Pour the sauce over fish and vegetables. Season with salt and pepper.
- Bake for about 15-20 minutes. Brushing with pan juices halfway through.
- Serve immediately and enjoy.

NUTRITIONAL INFORMATION

Energy	Fat	Carbohydrates	Protein	Sodium
317 calories	17.1 g	13.5 g	26.9 g	303 mg

BUTTERED SALMON WITH LEMON AND GARLIC

Preparation Time	Total Time	Yield
10 minutes	20 minutes	4 servings

INGREDIENTS

- 2 tablespoons (30 g) butter
- 1 teaspoon (3 g) garlic, minced
- 4 (5 oz. or 150 g) salmon fillets, boneless
- 2 tablespoons (30 ml) lemon juice
- Salt and freshly ground black pepper

METHOD

- Brush the salmon fillets with lemon juice and season with salt and pepper.
- Heat butter in a non-stick frying pan, stir-fry garlic for 2 minutes or until fragrant.
- Add the salmon fillets and cook for 3-4 minutes on each side or until golden and cooked through.
- Serve immediately and enjoy.

NUTRITIONAL INFORMATION

Energy	Fat	Carbohydrates	Protein	Sodium
268 calories	17.5 g	0.5 g	27.7 g	274 mg

PISTACHIO-CRUSTED SALMON

Preparation Time	Total Time	Yield
10 minutes	20 minutes	4 servings

INGREDIENTS

- 1/4 cup (25 g) pistachios, crushed
- 2 tablespoons (15 g) bread crumbs
- 1 tablespoon (7 g) Parmesan cheese
- 1 tablespoon (15 g) butter, melted
- 4 (4 oz. or 125 g) salmon fillets with skin, center cut
- 2 tablespoons (30 ml) olive oil
- 1 tablespoon (15 g) Dijon mustard
- 4 lemon wedges
- Salt and freshly ground black pepper

METHOD

- Preheat and set your oven to 380 F (190 C).
- Combine the butter, parmesan cheese, pistachios and bread crumbs in a shallow bowl; mix until combined well.
- Season your salmon fillets with salt and pepper.
- Heat the olive oil in a large skillet, sear the salmon fillets for 3 minutes, flesh-side down. Turn off the heat then flip the salmon pieces, putting skin side down. Brush the tops with Dijon mustard evenly.
- Coat each salmon with pistachio mixture and then place them in the preheated oven; cook until it flakes easily with a fork.

• Serve with lemon wedges and enjoy.

NUTRITIONAL INFORMATION

Energy	Fat	Carbohydrates	Protein	Sodium
328 calories	22 g	7.0 g	32 g	222 mg

MAPLE-SOY SALMON WITH SESAME

Preparation Time	Total Time	Yield
10 minutes	30 minutes	4 servings

INGREDIENTS

- 1/4 cup (80 ml) maple syrup
- 2 tablespoons (30 ml) soy sauce
- 1 teaspoon (3 g) garlic, minced
- 1/4 teaspoon (1.5 g) sea salt
- 1/4 teaspoon (0.5 g) ground black pepper
- 1 pound (450 g) salmon steak
- 1 tablespoon sesame seeds, toasted

METHOD

- In a mixing bowl, combine the maple syrup, soy sauce, garlic, salt, pepper.
- Put your salmon steak in a shallow baking dish, then coat with your prepared soy-maple mixture. Cover your baking dish and put in fridge for 30 minutes to absorb flavors.
- Preheat and set your oven to 400 F (200 C).
- Place the baking dish inside the preheated oven and bake your salmon steak for about 15 minutes or until it can be easily flaked with a fork. Sprinkle with toasted sesame seeds.
- Serve and enjoy.

NUTRITIONAL INFORMATION

Energy	Fat	Carbohydrates	Protein	Sodium
265 calories	13 g	14.0 g	23 g	633 mg

SALMON TIKKA BITES

Preparation Time	Total Time	Yield
10 minutes	30 minutes	2 servings

INGREDIENTS

- 2 teaspoons (4 g) ground red pepper or cayenne
- 1/2 teaspoon (1 g) ground turmeric
- 1/2 teaspoon (2.5 g) salt
- 1/2 pound (225 g) wild Pacific salmon fillets, cut into 1-inch cubes
- 2 teaspoons (5 g) cornstarch
- Vegetable oil for frying

METHOD

- Combine the turmeric, cayenne, and salt in a bowl. Add in the salmon and toss to coat with your dry ingredients. Leave it for about 15 minutes to absorb flavors.
- Heat the oil in a skillet or frying pan over medium-high flame.
- Sprinkle your salmon with cornstarch and toss again to coat.
- Cook the salmon in the heated oil until golden brown.
- Transfer to a serving dish.
- Serve and enjoy.

NUTRITIONAL INFORMATION

Energy	Fat	Carbohydrates	Protein	Sodium
229 calories	13 g	5.0 g	25 g	629 mg

POTATO SALMON PATTIES

Preparation Time	Total Time	Yield
15 minutes	45 minutes	5 servings

INGREDIENTS

- 1 (14.75 ounce) flaked canned salmon
- 2 large eggs (about 60 g each), beaten
- 1/4 cup (25 g) seasoned dry bread crumbs
- 1/4 cup (25 g) dry potato flakes
- 1 medium (110 g) onion, minced
- 1 teaspoon (3 g) garlic, minced
- 1/2 teaspoon (1 g) dried dill weed
- 1/2 teaspoon (1 g) ground coriander seeds
- 2 tablespoons (30 ml) olive oil
- Salt and freshly ground black pepper

METHOD

- In a medium bowl, combine the salmon, eggs, garlic and herb seasoned dry bread crumbs, dry potato flakes, onion, garlic, dill weed, and coriander. Season to taste.
- Form 2-inch balls from your mixture and then flatten to make them into patties that is ½-inch thick.
- Heat olive oil in a non-stick pan or skillet over medium-high flame. Cook the salmon patties about 5 minutes on each side or until golden brown.
- Transfer to a serving dish.
- Serve and enjoy.

NUTRITIONAL INFORMATION

Energy	Fat	Carbohydrates	Protein	Sodium
252 calories	14 g	10.0 g	23 g	509 mg

SOY GINGER SALMON

Preparation Time	Total Time	Yield
10 minutes	3 hours	4 servings

INGREDIENTS

- 2.2 pound (1 kg) salmon fillet
- 4 tablespoons (60 g) brown sugar, divided
- 2 teaspoons (4 g) garlic powder, divided
- 1 teaspoon (2 g) lemon pepper, divided
- 2 tablespoons (30 ml) low-sodium soy sauce
- 1 tablespoon (15 ml) soybean oil
- 1-inch (10 g) minced ginger root
- 1/3 cup (85 ml) orange juice

METHOD

- Rub the salmon with 1 tablespoon brown sugar, and then sprinkle with 1 teaspoon garlic powder and ½ teaspoon lemon pepper.
- In a small saucepan set over medium flame, add the soy sauce and oil. Stir in the remaining brown sugar, lemon pepper, garlic powder and ginger. Bring to a simmer while stirring frequently, cook for 3-5 minutes. Add the orange juice and mix well. Let it cool.
- Place your salmon together with the cooled marinade inside a resealable plastic bag, and keep in the fridge for at least 2 hours.
- Preheat your broiler. Remove salmon from the plastic bag and put in a foil-lined pan. Keep the marinade aside.
- Broil salmon skin-side up for about 3 minutes. Remove

from the oven and take off the skin with tongs. Brush with your marinade and put it back into the oven; broil for another 5 minutes or until cooked through.
- Transfer to a serving dish.
- Serve and enjoy.

NUTRITIONAL INFORMATION

Energy	Fat	Carbohydrates	Protein	Sodium
333 calories	16 g	23.0 g	24 g	364 mg

FURIKAKE SALMON

Preparation Time	Total Time	Yield
10 minutes	20 minutes	4 servings

INGREDIENTS

- 4 (4 oz. or 125 g) salmon steaks
- 1/2 teaspoon (2.5 g) garlic salt
- 1/4 teaspoon (0.5 g) ground black pepper
- 2 tablespoons (30 g) mayonnaise
- 2 teaspoons (15 ml) honey
- 1 container nori fumi furikake
- 2 tablespoons (30 ml) vegetable oil for frying

METHOD

- Season salmon steaks with garlic salt and black pepper.
- Mix the mayonnaise and honey together and brush on your salmon steaks.
- Dip top side of each salmon steak in Furikake. Remember to press lightly for coating to stick onto the salmon.
- Heat oil in a large skillet and place the salmon coated-side down. Let it cook until golden brown for about 5 minutes. Turn it over to continue cooking until salmon flakes easily with a fork.
- Serve and enjoy.

NUTRITIONAL INFORMATION

Energy	Fat	Carbohydrates	Protein	Sodium
300 calories	12 g	17.0 g	30 g	691 mg

SALMON WITH CARAMELIZED ONION

Preparation Time	Total Time	Yield
10 minutes	30 minutes	4 servings

INGREDIENTS

- 1/4 cup (60 g) butter
- 1 teaspoon (3 g) garlic, minced
- 4 (5 oz. or 150 g) salmon fillets
- 3 large onion about (150 g each), thinly sliced
- 1/4 cup (60 ml) white vinegar
- 1/4 cup (55 g) brown sugar

METHOD

- Preheat and set your oven to 350 F (175 C).
- Combine the onion, vinegar and brown sugar in a saucepan over medium flame. Continue stirring until the sauce begins to caramelize.
- Melt butter in a small skillet over medium flame, stir fry garlic for 1 minute.
- Place your salmon fillets on a baking dish and brush with garlic butter. Then, pour the onion mixture over salmon.
- Bake for 20 to 25 minutes in the preheated oven or until the fish flakes easily.
- Serve and enjoy.

NUTRITIONAL INFORMATION

Energy	Fat	Carbohydrates	Protein	Sodium
298 calories	11 g	23.0 g	23 g	117 mg

FETTUCCINI SALMON AND PEAS IN WHITE SAUCE

Preparation Time	Total Time	Yield
15 minutes	30 minutes	4 servings

INGREDIENTS

- 8 ounces (250 g) fettuccini, dry
- 2 tablespoons (30 g) butter
- 2 teaspoons (6 g) garlic, minced
- 1 medium (110 g) onion, chopped
- 10 ounces (300 g) canned pink salmon fillet, flaked
- 4 ounces (125 g) frozen green peas, thawed
- 1/4 cup (60 ml) white wine
- 2/3 cup (165 g) all-purpose cream
- 2/3 cup (165 ml) whole milk
- 1/2 teaspoon (1 g) dried sage
- 1/4 cup (30 g) parmesan cheese, grated
- Salt and freshly ground black pepper

METHOD

- Cook fettuccini in a stock pot with boiling salted water for 10-12 minutes. Drain and then set aside.
- Heat butter in a saucepan over medium flame, stir-fry garlic and onion until aromatic.
- Add the salmon, peas, and white wine; cook for 2 minutes.
- Add the cream, milk, and sage; cook for another 5

minutes, stirring frequently. Season with salt and pepper.

- Divide pasta among individual plates. Top with salmon and white sauce, and then sprinkle with parmesan.
- Serve immediately and enjoy.

NUTRITIONAL INFORMATION

Energy	Fat	Carbohydrates	Protein	Sodium
456 calories	16.5 g	53.5 g	23.8 g	429 mg

SALMON CHEESE AND PASTA CASSEROLE

Preparation Time	Total Time	Yield
15 minutes	30 minutes	5 servings

INGREDIENTS

- 1 pound (450 g) macaroni, dry
- 1 teaspoon (2 g) paprika
- 2 tablespoons (30 ml) olive oil
- 2 tablespoons (7 g) fresh basil
- 1 tablespoon (10 g) garlic, minced
- 1/4 cup (30 g) cheddar cheese, grated
- 1 medium (110 g) onion, chopped
- 1/4 cup (30 g) mozzarella cheese, grated
- 12 ounces (340 g) baked pink salmon, cut into pieces
- 1 medium (120 g) red bell pepper, chopped
- 1 cup (250 g) tomato sauce
- Salt and freshly ground black pepper
- Fresh basil or parsley, for garnish

METHOD

- Preheat and set your oven to 350 F (175 C).
- Boil your salted water in a large pot. Cook the macaroni for 10-12 minutes. Drain and set aside.
- Heat oil in a skillet over medium-high flame, stir-fry garlic and onion until fragrant.
- Add in bell pepper, paprika, tomato sauce, basil, and salmon. Cook for 5-7 minutes, stirring occasionally. Season with salt and pepper.

- Coat the macaroni noodles with the sauce and mix well. Transfer to a baking dish. Sprinkle with cheddar and mozzarella cheese.
- Bake for 15–20 minutes. Remove from heat and garnish with fresh basil or parsley.
- Serve and enjoy.

NUTRITIONAL INFORMATION

Energy	Fat	Carbohydrates	Protein	Sodium
380 calories	11.9 g	47.3 g	22.1 g	393 mg

LEMON GARLIC PASTA WITH SALMON

Preparation Time	Total Time	Yield
5 minutes	30 minutes	8 servings

INGREDIENTS

- 16 ounces (450 g) penne pasta
- 2 tablespoons (20 g) garlic, minced
- 1/4 cup (60 ml) olive oil
- 1/2 cup (30 g) basil leaves, chopped
- 1 pound (450 g) salmon fillet
- Zest of one lemon
- 1/4 cup (60 ml) lemon juice
- 2 teaspoons (10 g) capers
- Parmesan cheese, shaved or grated
- Salt and freshly ground black pepper

METHOD

- Boil and cook your pasta in a casserole filled with salted water until al dente, about 10-12 minutes.
- While waiting, season your salmon with salt and pepper, and then bake at 350 F (175 C) for 15 minutes.
- Once your pasta is ready, toss it with garlic, olive oil, and basil; season with salt and pepper.
- Stir in lemon juice and zest. Then, add in the capers and mix well.
- Flake the salmon and gently toss with the pasta.
- Serve while still hot and sprinkle with Parmesan cheese for added flavor.

NUTRITIONAL INFORMATION

Energy	Fat	Carbohydrates	Protein	Sodium
355 calories	10.8 g	43.5 g	23.1 g	179 mg

SALMON PASTA IN TOMATO SAUCE

Preparation Time	Total Time	Yield
5 minutes	20 minutes	6 servings

INGREDIENTS

- 1 package (16 oz. or 450 g) dry spaghetti
- 1/3 cup (85 ml) olive oil
- 2 tablespoons (20 g) garlic, minced
- 1 ½ cups (225 g) canned salmon, drained
- 1 ½ cups (375 g) tomato sauce
- 1 cup (250 ml) chicken broth
- 1/4 cup (15 g) fresh parsley, chopped
- 1 teaspoon (2 g) paprika
- 1 teaspoon (1 g) cayenne pepper
- 1/2 teaspoon (2.5 g) sea salt
- Parmesan cheese, to serve

METHOD

- Cook your spaghetti as directed in the package directions and drain.
- Heat oil in a large skillet and cook your salmon with garlic for 3 minutes.
- Add the tomato sauce, chicken broth, parsley, paprika, and cayenne; cook for 7-8 minutes.
- Add in your linguine and carefully toss until well combined. Season to taste.
- Transfer to a serving dish and sprinkle with Parmesan.
- Serve and enjoy.

NUTRITIONAL INFORMATION

Energy	Fat	Carbohydrates	Protein	Sodium
489 calories	19 g	56.0 g	25 g	693 mg

TUSCAN SALMON PASTA

Preparation Time	Total Time	Yield
5 minutes	20 minutes	2 servings

INGREDIENTS

- 4 ounces (125 g) uncooked fusilli pasta
- 1 (10 oz. or 300 g) salmon fillet, cut into 1-inch cubes
- 2 tablespoons (7 g) fresh rosemary
- 4 tablespoons (60 ml) olive oil, divided
- 3/4 cup (130 g) cannellini beans, rinsed and drained
- 2 small plum tomatoes (about 100 g each), chopped
- 1 tablespoon (10 g) garlic, minced
- Salt and freshly ground black pepper

METHOD

- Cook your pasta according to package directions.
- While waiting, sauté your salmon and rosemary in 2 tablespoons oil for 5 minutes
- Add the beans, tomatoes, and garlic; cook for 10 minutes.
- Drain the pasta, and then transfer to a large bowl. Add in your sautéed salmon and toss carefully. Drizzle with remaining oil and season to taste.
- Serve and enjoy.

NUTRITIONAL INFORMATION

Energy	Fat	Carbohydrates	Protein	Sodium
431 calories	25 g	32.0 g	21 g	215 mg

SALMON CASSEROLE WITH PECAN

Preparation Time	Total Time	Yield
20 minutes	50 minutes	12 servings

INGREDIENTS

- 1 package (16 oz. or 450 g) small shell pasta
- 2 medium onions (about 110 g each), finely chopped
- 1/2 pound (225 g) sliced fresh mushrooms
- 1/4 cup (60 g) butter, cubed
- 2 cans cream of mushroom soup
- 1-1/2 cups (375 ml) milk
- 1 tablespoon (15 ml) Worcestershire sauce
- 1 teaspoon (5 g) sea salt
- 1/2 teaspoon (1 g) ground black pepper
- 2 cups (300 g) canned salmon (drained and skin removed)
- 2 cups (340 g) frozen peas
- 1 cup (100 g) chopped pecans, toasted
- 1/2 cup (80 g) diced pimiento (drained)
- 1 cup (30 g) crushed cornflakes

METHOD

- Cook your pasta according to package directions.
- Use a skillet to sauté onions and mushrooms in butter until tender. Stir in milk, mushroom soup, Worcestershire sauce, salt, and pepper, then bring to boil.
- Drain the cooked pasta and put it into the skillet with mushroom sauce. Add your salmon, peas, pecans,

and pimiento into the skillet as well. Toss to combine.
- Transfer everything to a large greased baking dish.
- Bake at 400 F (200 C) for 20 minutes.
- Sprinkle with cornflakes and serve.

NUTRITIONAL INFORMATION

Energy	Fat	Carbohydrates	Protein	Sodium
295 calories	17 g	24.0 g	14 g	668 mg

SALMON MACARONI BAKE

Preparation Time	Total Time	Yield
20 minutes	50 minutes	4 servings

INGREDIENTS

- 1 package (14 oz. or 420 g) macaroni and cheese dinner mix
- 1 can cream of mushroom soup
- 1/2 cup (125 ml) low-fat milk
- 1 cup (150 g) canned salmon, drained and flaked
- 1/2 teaspoon (1 g) onion powder
- 1/2 cup (60 g) shredded cheddar cheese
- 1/2 cup (50 g) dry bread crumbs
- 2 tablespoons (30 g) butter, melted

METHOD

- Cook the macaroni and cheese as per package directions.
- Stir in salmon, cream of mushroom soup, milk, onion powder, and cheddar cheese. Transfer to a greased baking dish. Sprinkle with bread crumbs on top and dot with butter.
- Bake at 400 F (200 C) for 20 minutes. Do not cover.
- Cool slightly before serving.
- Enjoy.

NUTRITIONAL INFORMATION

Energy	Fat	Carbohydrates	Protein	Sodium
599 calories	27 g	62.0 g	28 g	748 mg

PASTA WITH SALMON AND CHERRY TOMATOES

Preparation Time	Total Time	Yield
10 minutes	25 minutes	6 servings

INGREDIENTS

- 1 (16 oz. 450 g) package spaghetti
- 2 tablespoons (30 ml) olive oil
- 10 ounces (300 g) salmon fillet, cut into cubes
- 1 teaspoon (3 g) garlic, minced
- 1 pound (450 g) cherry tomatoes, quartered
- 1/4 cup (15 g) chopped fresh basil
- 3/4 cup (185 g) heavy cream
- Salt and freshly ground black pepper

METHOD

- Add lightly salted water into a large pot and bring to a boil. Cook the spaghetti in boiling water for about 12 minutes, and then drain.
- Heat oil in a skillet over medium flame, cook garlic until aromatic and lightly browned.
- Add the salmon, tomatoes, and basil; cook, stirring for 5-7 minutes.
- Stir in cream and let it simmer for 7-8 minutes.
- Divide the pasta among individual plates and top with sauce.
- Serve and enjoy.

NUTRITIONAL INFORMATION

Energy	Fat	Carbohydrates	Protein	Sodium
466 calories	16 g	60.0 g	20 g	67 mg

PASTA WITH SALMON AND SPINACH IN WHITE SAUCE

Preparation Time	Total Time	Yield
15 minutes	30 minutes	6 servings

INGREDIENTS

- 1 pound (450 g) spiral pasta, dry
- 2 tablespoons (30 g) butter
- 1 tablespoon (10 g) garlic, minced
- 1 shallot (about 40 g), chopped
- 12 oz. (340 g) canned pink salmon, flaked
- 1/4 cup (60 ml) dry white wine
- 1 cup (250 g) all-purpose cream
- 6 ounces (185 g) baby spinach
- 1 tablespoon (3.5 g) fresh basil, chopped
- 2 tablespoons (15 g) parmesan cheese

METHOD

- Cook pasta in a large saucepan with salted boiling water as directed on the package. Drain and set aside.
- Heat butter in a large skillet over medium flame, stir-fry garlic and shallot until fragrant.
- Add the salmon and dry white wine; cook for 3 minutes.
- Add the cream, spinach, and basil; cook for 4-5 minutes, stirring frequently. Season with salt and pepper.
- Add the pasta and toss to coat with sauce. Cook

for another 2 minutes. Divide among serving plates. Sprinkle with parmesan cheese.
- Enjoy!

NUTRITIONAL INFORMATION

Energy	Fat	Carbohydrates	Protein	Sodium
483 calories	15.1 g	59.4 g	24.3 g	230 mg

SALAD
RECIPES

SALMON PASTA AND BROCCOLI SALAD

Preparation Time	Total Time	Yield
15 minutes	15 minutes	6 servings

INGREDIENTS

- 4 cups (480 g) cooked penne pasta
- 2 cups (240 g) broccoli florets, steamed
- 1 cup (120 g) feta cheese, diced
- 6 ounces (180 g) smoked salmon, diced
- 1 teaspoon (3 g) red peppercorns
- Salt and freshly ground black pepper

Dressing:

- 1/3 cup (85 ml) olive oil
- 1/4 cup (60 ml) balsamic vinegar
- 1 tablespoon (20 ml) honey
- 1 teaspoon fresh dill weed, chopped

METHOD

- In a large bowl, combine the penne, broccoli, feta, smoked salmon, and peppercorns. Season to taste and set aside.
- Whisk all dressing ingredients (olive oil, balsamic vinegar, honey and dill) in a small bowl. Pour this mixture into the salad and toss to coat.
- Divide among 6 individual bowls.
- Serve and enjoy.

NUTRITIONAL INFORMATION

Energy	Fat	Carbohydrates	Protein	Sodium
356 calories	19.3 g	29.0 g	16.6 g	319 mg

TABBOULEH SALAD WITH SALMON AND CUCUMBER

Preparation Time	Total Time	Yield
15 minutes	15 minutes	3 servings

INGREDIENTS

- 1 cup (180 g) cracked wheat or bulgur, cooked
- 6 ounces (180 g) baked pink salmon, flaked
- 1 cup (150 g) cherry tomatoes, halved
- 1/2 medium (100 g) cucumber, thinly sliced
- 1 cup (60 g) flat-leaf parsley, chopped
- 1/2 cup (30 g) fresh mint leaves, chopped
- 1/2 cup (30 g) green onion, chopped
- 2 tablespoons (30 ml) lemon juice
- 2 tablespoons (30 ml) olive oil
- Salt and freshly ground black pepper

METHOD

- Combine the cracked wheat, salmon, cherry tomatoes, cucumber, parsley, mint, and green onion in a medium bowl. Drizzle with lemon juice and olive oil. Toss to combine well. Season to taste.
- Transfer to a serving dish.
- Serve and enjoy.

NUTRITIONAL INFORMATION

Energy	Fat	Carbohydrates	Protein	Sodium
312 calories	13.8 g	34.1 g	17.5 g	248 mg

GRILLED SALMON WITH CAESAR SALAD

Preparation Time	Total Time	Yield
15 minutes	30 minutes	4 servings

INGREDIENTS

- 4 (4 oz. or 125 g) salmon fillet, with skin
- 1 tablespoon (15 ml) olive oil
- 1/2 teaspoon (1 g) dried sage
- 1/4 teaspoon (1.5 g) sea salt
- 1/4 teaspoon (0.5 g) freshly ground black pepper
- 10 ounces (300 g) Romaine lettuce leaves
- 4 ounces (125 g) croutons, herbed
- 1/4 cup (60 g) Caesar salad dressing
- 1/4 cup (30 g) Parmesan cheese, grated

METHOD

- Preheat your grill to high.
- Rub salmon with oil and sage. Season with salt and pepper.
- Grill the salmon for about 3-4 minutes on each side, turning halfway through cooking until grill marks form and just cooked.
- Meanwhile, divide the lettuce into serving plates and top with croutons. Drizzle with dressing on top and sprinkle with Parmesan cheese.
- Serve grilled salmon on the side or on top of salad.
- Enjoy.

NUTRITIONAL INFORMATION

Energy	Fat	Carbohydrates	Protein	Sodium
434 calories	23.3 g	26.9 g	30.8 g	345 mg

SALMON AND POTATO SALAD

Preparation Time	Total Time	Yield
15 minutes	15 minutes	6 servings

INGREDIENTS

- 12 ounces (340 g) oven-roasted pink salmon fillet, flaked
- 1 pound (450 g) cooked potatoes, unpeeled and quartered
- 2 hard-boiled eggs (about 60 g each), chopped
- 1/2 medium (100 g) cucumber, cut into small pieces
- 8 (8 g) kalamata olives, sliced
- 1 shallot (about 40 g), chopped
- 1/3 cup (85 g) mayonnaise
- 1/3 cup (85 g) Greek yogurt
- Salt and freshly ground black pepper

METHOD

- Combine the salmon, potatoes, eggs, cucumber, olives, shallot, mayonnaise, and yogurt in a large bowl. Season with salt and pepper. Toss to combine and coat well. Cover and chill until the salad is ready to serve.
- Transfer to a serving dish and garnish with some cucumber slices and olives, if desired.
- Serve and enjoy.

NUTRITIONAL INFORMATION

Energy	Fat	Carbohydrates	Protein	Sodium
382 calories	18.5 g	28.8 g	25.1 g	314 mg

PASTA SALMON AND CORN SALAD

Preparation Time	Total Time	Yield
15 minutes	15 minutes	4 servings

INGREDIENTS

- 2 cups (200 g) penne, cooked
- 10 ounces (300 g) canned salmon fillet, drained and flaked
- 1 cup (165 g) sweet corn kernels
- 1 medium (120 g) bell red pepper, chopped

Balsamic Vinaigrette Dressing:

- 1/4 cup (60 ml) extra-virgin olive oil
- 2 tablespoons (30 ml) balsamic vinegar
- 1/4 teaspoon (0.5 g) dried thyme
- 1/4 teaspoon (0.5 g) dried sage
- Salt and freshly ground black pepper

METHOD

- Whisk together the oil, balsamic vinegar, thyme, and sage in a small glass bowl. Set aside.
- Combine the penne, salmon, corn, and pepper in a large mixing bowl. Drizzle with balsamic vinaigrette and season to taste. Toss to combine well.
- Divide among serving plates.
- Serve and enjoy.

NUTRITIONAL INFORMATION

Energy	Fat	Carbohydrates	Protein	Sodium
352 calories	16 g	31.0 g	16.4 g	274 mg

SALMON MACARONI SALAD

Preparation Time	Total Time	Yield
20 minutes	20 minutes	4 servings

INGREDIENTS

- 12 ounces (340 g) oven-roasted pink salmon fillet, flaked
- 10 ounces (300 g) macaroni, dry
- 1/2 medium (55 g) onion, finely chopped
- 2 celery stalks (about 60 g each), chopped
- 3/4 cup (185 g) mayonnaise
- 2 tablespoons (30 g) Dijon mustard
- 1 tablespoon (15 ml) lemon juice
- Salt and freshly ground black pepper

METHOD

- Cook the macaroni as directed in the package cooking instructions. Drain and set aside.
- In a small bowl, mix together mayonnaise, Dijon mustard, and lemon juice.
- Combine the salmon, macaroni, onion, celery, and dressing in a large bowl. Season to taste and toss to coat well.
- Cover and place in the fridge until ready to serve.
- Enjoy.

NUTRITIONAL INFORMATION

Energy	Fat	Carbohydrates	Protein	Sodium
389 calories	16.7 g	31.5 g	26.4 g	477 mg

SALMON CUCUMBER AND TOMATO SALAD

Preparation Time	Total Time	Yield
15 minutes	15 minutes	4 servings

INGREDIENTS

- 10 ounces (300 g) smoked salmon fillet, cut into small pieces
- 1 medium (200 g) cucumber, thinly sliced
- 2 cups (300 g) cherry tomatoes, halved
- 1 tablespoon (3.5 g) dill weed, chopped
- 1 cup (30 g) croutons
- Salt and freshly ground black pepper
- Fresh parsley, to serve

For Red Wine Vinaigrette:

- 1/4 cup (60 ml) olive oil
- 2 tablespoons (30 ml) red wine vinegar
- 1 tablespoon honey

METHOD

- In a small mixing bowl, whisk together the olive oil, red wine vinegar, and honey. Set aside.
- Combine the salmon, cucumber, tomatoes, dill, and croutons in a mixing bowl. Season to taste and then toss to combine.
- Transfer to a serving dish. Drizzle with red wine vinaigrette and garnish with fresh parsley.
- Serve and enjoy.

NUTRITIONAL INFORMATION

Energy	Fat	Carbohydrates	Protein	Sodium
289 calories	18.9 g	18.0 g	15.4 g	599 mg

MEDITERRANEAN SALMON SALAD

Preparation Time	Total Time	Yield
15 minutes	15 minutes	4 servings

INGREDIENTS

- 12 ounces (340 g) oven-roasted pink salmon fillet, flaked
- 1 head (350 g) Romaine lettuce, torn
- 1 cup (150 g) feta cheese
- 1 cup (150 g) grape tomatoes
- 4 ounces (120 g) pitted black olives, drained
- 1/4 cup (15 g) flat-leaf parsley, chopped

For Balsamic Vinaigrette:

- 1/4 cup (60 ml) olive oil
- 2 tablespoons (30 ml) balsamic vinegar
- 1 tablespoon (15 g) Dijon mustard

METHOD

- In a small mixing bowl, whisk together all ingredients for the balsamic vinaigrette and set aside.
- Place the salmon, lettuce, feta cheese, tomatoes, olives, and parsley in a large mixing bowl. Season to taste and then toss to combine.
- Transfer to a serving dish and drizzle with balsamic vinaigrette.
- Serve and enjoy.

NUTRITIONAL INFORMATION

Energy	Fat	Carbohydrates	Protein	Sodium
363 calories	26.7 g	8.5 g	23.6 g	482 mg

SALMON ORANGE AND ARUGULA SALAD

Preparation Time	Total Time	Yield
15 minutes	15 minutes	4 servings

INGREDIENTS

- 8 ounces (250 g) oven-roasted pink salmon fillet, cut into small pieces
- 2 oranges (about 150 g each), peeled and cut into segments
- 1 cup (150 g) cherry tomato, halved
- 8 ounces (250 g) arugula or baby rocket
- 3 tablespoons (45 ml) olive oil
- 3 tablespoons (45 ml) balsamic vinegar
- Salt and freshly ground black pepper

METHOD

- Place the salmon, orange segments, tomatoes, and arugula in a salad bowl. Toss to combine and season to taste.
- Transfer to a serving dish and drizzle with oil and balsamic vinegar.
- Serve and enjoy.

NUTRITIONAL INFORMATION

Energy	Fat	Carbohydrates	Protein	Sodium
255 calories	17.5 g	9.5 g	15.8 g	188 mg

GARDEN FRESH SALAD WITH SALMON

Preparation Time	Total Time	Yield
15 minutes	15 minutes	4 servings

INGREDIENTS

- 8 ounces (250 g) oven-roasted pink salmon fillet, cut into small pieces
- 1 medium (200 g) cucumber, thinly sliced
- 1 cup (150 g) cherry tomatoes, halved
- 3 cups (180 g) baby spinach
- 3 cups (150 g) red lettuce, shredded
- 3 tablespoons (45 ml) olive oil
- 3 tablespoons (45 ml) lemon juice
- 1 tablespoon (20 ml) honey
- Salt and freshly ground black pepper

METHOD

- In a small bowl, whisk together oil, lemon juice, and honey. Set aside.
- Place the salmon, cucumber, tomatoes, spinach, and lettuce in a mixing bowl. Toss to combine and season with salt and pepper.
- Transfer to a serving dish and drizzle with prepared dressing.
- Serve and enjoy.

NUTRITIONAL INFORMATION

Energy	Fat	Carbohydrates	Protein	Sodium
257 calories	17.5 g	9.7 g	16.0 g	209 mg

SALMON PASTA SALAD WITH YOGURT-HERB DRESSING

Preparation Time	Total Time	Yield
15 minutes	15 minutes	4 servings

INGREDIENTS

- 2 cups (240 g) rigati or penne pasta, cooked
- 8 ounces (250 g) canned pink salmon, drained and flaked
- 1 medium (120 g) red bell pepper, chopped
- 2 celery stalks (about 60 g each), thinly sliced
- 1/4 cup (15 g) fresh parsley, chopped

Yogurt-Herb Dressing:

- 6 ounces (185 g) Greek yogurt
- 2 tablespoons (30 ml) lemon juice
- 1/4 teaspoon (0.5 g) sage, dried
- 1/4 teaspoon (0.5 g) parsley, dried
- Salt and freshly ground black pepper

METHOD

- Whisk together the yogurt, lemon juice, sage, and dried parsley in a small glass bowl. Set aside.
- Combine the macaroni, salmon, bell pepper, and celery in a large mixing bowl. Season with salt and pepper. Toss to combine well.
- Divide among individual plates. Drizzle with yogurt-herb dressing. Sprinkle with fresh parsley.
- Serve and enjoy.

NUTRITIONAL INFORMATION

Energy	Fat	Carbohydrates	Protein	Sodium
314 calories	6.3 g	39.0 g	25.0 g	213 mg

SALMON MACARONI AND SULTANA SALAD

Preparation Time	Total Time	Yield
15 minutes	15 minutes	4 servings

INGREDIENTS

- 4 cups (480 g) macaroni, cooked
- 10 ounces (300 g) canned pink salmon fillet, flaked
- 2 celery stalks (about 60 g each), chopped
- 1/2 cup (60 g) seedless sultanas
- 1/4 cup (15 g) green onion, chopped
- 1/2 cup (125 g) mayonnaise
- 1/2 cup (125 g) Greek yogurt
- 1/4 cup (30 g) cheddar cheese, grated
- Salt and freshly ground black pepper

METHOD

- Mix together the mayonnaise and yogurt in a small bowl.
- Combine the macaroni, salmon, celery, sultanas, and green onion in a large bowl.
- Add the dressing and cheese. Toss to coat, and then season with salt and pepper.
- Transfer to a container with lid. Cover and keep in the fridge until ready to serve.
- Enjoy.

NUTRITIONAL INFORMATION

Energy	Fat	Carbohydrates	Protein	Sodium
376 calories	14.2 g	40.2 g	24.6 g	292 mg

BREAKFAST &
SNACK RECIPES

GRILLED SALMON BURGER

Preparation Time	Total Time	Yield
15 minutes	25 minutes	4 servings

INGREDIENTS

- 16 ounces (450 g) pink salmon fillet, minced
- 1 cup (250 g) prepared mashed potatoes
- 1 shallot (about 40 g), chopped
- 1 large egg (about 60 g), lightly beaten
- 2 tablespoons (7 g) fresh coriander, chopped
- 4 Hamburger buns (about 60 g each), split
- 1 large tomato (about 150 g), sliced
- 8 (15 g) Romaine lettuce leaves
- 1/4 cup (60 g) mayonnaise
- Salt and freshly ground black pepper
- Cooking oil spray

METHOD

- Combine the salmon, mashed potatoes, shallot, egg, and coriander in a mixing bowl. Season with salt and pepper.
- Spoon about 2 tablespoons of mixture and form into patties.
- Preheat your grill or griddle on high. Grease with cooking oil spray.
- Grill the salmon patties for 4-5 minutes on each side or until cooked through. Transfer to a clean plate and cover to keep warm.

- Spread some mayonnaise on the bottom half of buns. Top with lettuce, salmon patty, and tomato. Cover with bun tops.
- Serve and enjoy.

NUTRITIONAL INFORMATION

Energy	Fat	Carbohydrates	Protein	Sodium
395 calories	18.0 g	38.8 g	21.8 g	383 mg

EASY SALMON BURGER

Preparation Time	Total Time	Yield
15 minutes	30 minutes	6 servings

INGREDIENTS

- 16 ounces (450 g) pink salmon, minced
- 1 cup (250 g) prepared mashed potatoes
- 1 medium (110 g) onion, chopped
- 1 stalk celery (about 60 g), finely chopped
- 1 large egg (about 60 g), lightly beaten
- 2 tablespoons (7 g) fresh cilantro, chopped
- 1 cup (100 g) breadcrumbs
- Vegetable oil, for deep frying
- Salt and freshly ground black pepper

METHOD

- Combine the salmon, mashed potatoes, onion, celery, egg, and cilantro in a mixing bowl. Season to taste and mix thoroughly. Spoon about 2 Tbsp. mixture, roll in breadcrumbs, and then form into small patties.
- Heat oil in non-stick frying pan. Cook your salmon patties for 5 minutes on each side or until golden brown and crispy.
- Serve in burger buns and with coleslaw on the side if desired.
- Enjoy.

NUTRITIONAL INFORMATION

Energy	Fat	Carbohydrates	Protein	Sodium
230 calories	7.9 g	20.9 g	18.9 g	298 mg

SALMON SANDWICH WITH AVOCADO AND EGG

Preparation Time	Total Time	Yield
15 minutes	15 minutes	4 servings

INGREDIENTS

- 8 ounces (250 g) smoked salmon, thinly sliced
- 1 medium (200 g) ripe avocado, thinly sliced
- 4 large poached eggs (about 60 g each)
- 4 slices whole wheat bread (about 30 g each)
- 2 cups (60 g) arugula or baby rocket
- Salt and freshly ground black pepper

METHOD

- Place 1 bread slice on a plate, top with arugula, avocado, salmon, and poached egg. Season with salt and pepper. Repeat procedure for the remaining ingredients.
- Serve and enjoy.

NUTRITIONAL INFORMATION

Energy	Fat	Carbohydrates	Protein	Sodium
310 calories	18.2 g	16.4 g	21.3 g	383 mg

SALMON SPINACH AND COTTAGE CHEESE SANDWICH

Preparation Time	Total Time	Yield
15 minutes	15 minutes	4 servings

INGREDIENTS

- 4 ounces (125 g) cottage cheese
- 1/4 cup (15 g) chives, chopped
- 1 teaspoon (5 g) capers
- 1/2 teaspoon (2.5 g) grated lemon rind
- 4 (2 oz. or 60 g) smoked salmon
- 2 cups (60 g) loose baby spinach
- 1 medium (110 g) red onion, sliced thinly
- 8 slices rye bread (about 30 g each)
- Kosher salt and freshly ground black pepper

METHOD

- Preheat your griddle or panini press.
- Mix together cottage cheese, chives, capers, and lemon rind in a small bowl.
- Spread and divide the cheese mixture on 4 bread slices. Top with spinach, onion slices, and smoked salmon.
- Cover with remaining bread slices.
- Grill the sandwiches until golden and grill marks form on both sides.
- Transfer to a serving dish.

- Serve and enjoy.

NUTRITIONAL INFORMATION

Energy	Fat	Carbohydrates	Protein	Sodium
261 calories	9.9 g	22.9 g	19.9 g	1226 mg

SALMON FETA AND PESTO WRAP

Preparation Time	Total Time	Yield
15 minutes	15 minutes	4 servings

INGREDIENTS

- 8 ounces (250 g) smoked salmon fillet, thinly sliced
- 1 cup (150 g) feta cheese
- 8 (15 g) Romaine lettuce leaves
- 4 (6-inch) pita bread
- 1/4 cup (60 g) basil pesto sauce

METHOD

- Place 1 pita bread on a plate. Top with lettuce, salmon, feta cheese, and pesto sauce. Fold or roll to enclose filling. Repeat procedure for the remaining ingredients.
- Serve and enjoy.

NUTRITIONAL INFORMATION

Energy	Fat	Carbohydrates	Protein	Sodium
379 calories	17.7 g	36.6 g	18.4 g	554 mg

SALMON CREAM CHEESE AND ONION ON BAGEL

Preparation Time	Total Time	Yield
15 minutes	15 minutes	4 servings

INGREDIENTS

- 8 ounces (250 g) smoked salmon fillet, thinly sliced
- 1/2 cup (125 g) cream cheese
- 1 medium (110 g) onion, thinly sliced
- 4 bagels (about 80g each), split
- 2 tablespoons (7 g) fresh parsley, chopped
- Freshly ground black pepper, to taste

METHOD

- Spread the cream cheese on each bottom half of bagels. Top with salmon and onion. Season with pepper, sprinkle with parsley, and then cover with bagel tops.
- Serve and enjoy.

NUTRITIONAL INFORMATION

Energy	Fat	Carbohydrates	Protein	Sodium
309 calories	14.1 g	32.0 g	14.7 g	571 mg

SALMON ROE AND GREEK YOGURT CANAPE

Preparation Time	Total Time	Yield
15 minutes	15 minutes	8 servings

INGREDIENTS

- 1 (8 oz. or 250 g) whole baguette
- 4 ounces (125 g) salmon roe (red caviar)
- 6 ounces (180 g) Greek yogurt, plain
- 1 tablespoon (15 ml) lemon juice
- 1 teaspoon (3 g) lemon zest, finely grated
- 2 tablespoons (7 g) green onion, finely chopped
- Salt and freshly ground black pepper
- Romaine lettuce leaves, to serve

METHOD

- Cut the baguette into 1-inch slices (horizontally). Set aside.
- In a small bowl, mix together yogurt, lemon juice, zest, and green onion. Season with salt and pepper.
- Spread the yogurt mixture onto the bread slices and top with salmon roe.
- Arrange the lettuce leaves in a serving platter to make a bed. Top with prepared salmon canapé.
- Serve and enjoy.

NUTRITIONAL INFORMATION

Energy	Fat	Carbohydrates	Protein	Sodium
101 calories	1.9 g	14.0 g	7.6 g	229 mg

SALMON SOUR CREAM AND CHIVES SANDWICH

Preparation Time	Total Time	Yield
15 minutes	15 minutes	4 servings

INGREDIENTS

- 8 ounces (250 g) smoked salmon fillet, thinly sliced
- 1/2 cup (125 g) sour cream
- 1/4 cup (15 g) fresh chives, chopped
- 8 (15 g) Romaine lettuce leaves
- 8 (20 g) onion slices
- 4 whole grain bun or sandwich roll (about 60 g each), split
- Salt and freshly ground black pepper

METHOD

- Mix together sour cream and chives in a small bowl. Season with salt and pepper.
- Spread the sour cream mixture on each bottom half of buns. Top with lettuce, onion, and salmon. Then cover with bun tops.
- Serve and enjoy.

NUTRITIONAL INFORMATION

Energy	Fat	Carbohydrates	Protein	Sodium
229 calories	11.7 g	21.1 g	11.7 g	443 mg

SALMON APPLE SALAD SANDWICH

Preparation Time	Total Time	Yield
15 minutes	15 minutes	4 servings

INGREDIENTS

- 4 ounces (125 g) canned pink salmon, drained and flaked
- 1 medium (180 g) red apple, cored and diced
- 1 celery stalk (about 60 g), chopped
- 1 shallot (about 40 g), finely chopped
- 1/3 cup (85 g) light mayonnaise
- 8 slices whole grain bread (about 30 g each), toasted
- 8 (15 g) Romaine lettuce leaves
- Salt and freshly ground black pepper

METHOD

- Combine the salmon, apple, celery, shallot, and mayonnaise in a mixing bowl. Season with salt and pepper.
- Place 1 slice bread on a plate, top with lettuce and salmon salad, and then cover with another slice of bread. Repeat procedure for the remaining ingredients.
- Serve and enjoy.

NUTRITIONAL INFORMATION

Energy	Fat	Carbohydrates	Protein	Sodium
305 calories	11.3 g	40.4 g	15.1 g	469 mg

SMOKED SALMON AND CHEESE ON RYE BREAD

Preparation Time	Total Time	Yield
15 minutes	15 minutes	4 servings

INGREDIENTS

- 8 ounces (250 g) smoked salmon, thinly sliced
- 1/3 cup (85 g) mayonnaise
- 2 tablespoons (30 ml) lemon juice
- 1 tablespoon (15 g) Dijon mustard
- 1 teaspoon (3 g) garlic, minced
- 4 slices cheddar cheese (about 2 oz. or 30 g each)
- 8 slices rye bread (about 2 oz. or 30 g each)
- 8 (15 g) Romaine lettuce leaves
- Salt and freshly ground black pepper

METHOD

- Mix together the mayonnaise, lemon juice, mustard, and garlic in a small bowl. Season with salt and pepper and set aside.
- Spread dressing on 4 bread slices. Top with lettuce, salmon, and cheese. Cover with remaining rye bread slices.
- Serve and enjoy.

NUTRITIONAL INFORMATION

Energy	Fat	Carbohydrates	Protein	Sodium
365 calories	16.6 g	31.6 g	18.8 g	951 mg

SALMON CUCUMBER AND ARUGULA SANDWICH

Preparation Time	Total Time	Yield
15 minutes	15 minutes	4 servings

INGREDIENTS

- 8 ounces (250 g) smoked salmon, thinly sliced
- 1 medium (200 g) cucumber, thinly sliced
- 1/3 cup (85 g) mayonnaise
- 1 tablespoon (15 ml) lemon juice
- 1 teaspoon (3 g) garlic, minced
- 2 tablespoons (7 g) parsley, finely chopped
- 8 slices white or whole wheat bread (about 2 oz. or 30 g each)
- 1 cup (60 g) arugula or baby rocket, packed
- Salt and freshly ground black pepper

METHOD

- Mix together mayonnaise, lemon juice, garlic, and parsley in a small bowl. Season with salt and pepper. Set aside.
- Divide the prepared dressing on 4 bread slices. Top with arugula, salmon, and cucumber. Cover with remaining bread slices.
- Serve and enjoy.

NUTRITIONAL INFORMATION

Energy	Fat	Carbohydrates	Protein	Sodium
287 calories	12.1 g	31.6 g	14.6 g	751 mg

SMOKED SALMON WITH DILL ON BURGER BUN

Preparation Time	Total Time	Yield
15 minutes	15 minutes	4 servings

INGREDIENTS

- 8 ounces (250 g) smoked salmon, thinly sliced
- 1/3 cup (85 g) mayonnaise
- 1 tablespoon (15 ml) lemon juice
- 1 shallot (about 40 g), minced
- 2 tablespoons (7 g) dill weed, chopped
- 4 Hamburger buns (about 60 g each)
- 8 (15 g) Romaine lettuce leaves
- Salt and freshly ground black pepper

METHOD

- Mix together the mayonnaise, lemon juice, shallot, and dill in a small bowl. Season with salt and pepper and set aside.
- Divide the prepared dressing on bottom half of buns. Top with lettuce and salmon, and then cover with bun tops.
- Serve and enjoy.

NUTRITIONAL INFORMATION

Energy	Fat	Carbohydrates	Protein	Sodium
272 calories	12.1 g	30.6 g	11.6 g	695 mg

SALMON CAPERS AND PARSLEY ON BAGEL

Preparation Time	Total Time	Yield
15 minutes	15 minutes	4 servings

INGREDIENTS

- 8 ounces (250 g) smoked salmon fillet, thinly sliced
- 1/2 cup (125 g) cream cheese
- 1/4 cup (15 g) fresh parsley, chopped
- 2 tablespoons (20 g) capers, drained
- 4 bagels (about 80 g each), split
- Freshly ground black pepper, to taste

METHOD

- Spread the cream cheese on each bottom half of bagels. Top with salmon and capers. Sprinkle with parsley. Season with pepper and then cover with bagel tops.
- Serve and enjoy.

NUTRITIONAL INFORMATION

Energy	Fat	Carbohydrates	Protein	Sodium
314 calories	13.8 g	36.1 g	12.7 g	622 mg

SALMON SALAD ON TOAST

Preparation Time	Total Time	Yield
20 minutes	20 minutes	4 servings

INGREDIENTS

- 1 (8 oz. or 250 g) whole baguette
- 8 ounces (250 g) smoked salmon, thinly sliced
- 6 ounces (180 g) Greek yogurt, plain
- 1 tablespoon (15 ml) lemon juice
- 1 teaspoon (3 g) lemon zest, finely grated
- 1 celery stalk (about 60 g), chopped
- 1 medium (60 g) carrot, chopped
- 2 tablespoons (7 g) dill weed, chopped
- Salt and freshly ground black pepper

METHOD

- Cut baguette into 1-inch slices (horizontally). Place in a toaster oven and cook on medium-high heat until golden. Set aside.
- Chop half of salmon and place in a mixing bowl. Add yogurt, lemon juice, zest, celery, carrot, and dill. Season with salt and pepper, to taste. Mix well.
- Spread yogurt mixture onto the toasted bread slices and top with remaining salmon.
- Serve and enjoy.

NUTRITIONAL INFORMATION

Energy	Fat	Carbohydrates	Protein	Sodium
237 calories	5.4 g	24.8 g	17.1 g	683 mg

HERBED SALMON AND CREAM CHEESE SPREAD

Preparation Time	Total Time	Yield
15 minutes	15 minutes	4 servings

INGREDIENTS

- 6 ounces (180 g) cooked salmon fillet, finely chopped
- 1 medium (60 g) carrot, finely chopped
- 1/2 medium (100 g) cucumber, finely chopped
- 1 celery stalk (about 60 g), finely chopped
- 1/3 cup (85 g) cream cheese
- 1/3 cup (85 g) Greek vanilla yogurt
- 2 tablespoons (7 g) fresh dill, chopped
- Bread toasts, to serve

METHOD

- In a large mixing bowl, combine the cream cheese and yogurt.
- Add the salmon, carrot, cucumber, celery, and dill. Mix well and season to taste.
- Transfer to a serving dish.
- Serve with bread toasts.
- Enjoy.

NUTRITIONAL INFORMATION

Energy	Fat	Carbohydrates	Protein	Sodium
299 calories	14.1 g	12.2 g	20.3 g	332 mg

RECIPE INDEX

L

Lemon Garlic Pasta with Salmon 88

M

Maple-Soy Salmon with Sesame 72
Mediterranean Salmon Salad 118

P

Pan-Fried Salmon with Mixed Vegetables 64
Pan-Fried Salmon with Potatoes and Herbs 18
Pasta Salmon and Corn Salad 112
Pasta with Salmon and Cherry Tomatoes 98
Pasta with Salmon and Spinach in White Sauce 100
Pistachio-Crusted Salmon 70
Poached Salmon with Lemon 46
Potato Salmon Patties 76

R

Risotto with Salmon and Peas 16
Roasted Salmon and Asparagus with Pesto 28
Roasted Salmon and Veggies 66

S

Salmon and Cherry Tomato Quiche 8
Salmon and Cottage Cheese Patties with Chives 48
Salmon and Potato Salad 110
Salmon and Tomato Omelette with Parsley 12
Salmon and Veggie Burger Patties 50
Salmon and Zucchini Risotto 14
Salmon Apple Salad Sandwich 146
Salmon Broccoli and Feta Quiche 6
Salmon Capers and Parsley on Bagel 154
Salmon Casserole with Pecan 94
Salmon Cheese and Pasta Casserole 86
Salmon Cream Cheese and Onion on Bagel 140
Salmon Cucumber and Arugula Sandwich 150
Salmon Cucumber and Tomato Salad 116
Salmon Feta and Pesto Wrap 138
Salmon Kebabs with Lemon and Rosemary 38

Salmon Macaroni and Sultana Salad 126
Salmon Macaroni Bake 96
Salmon Macaroni Salad 114
Salmon Mushroom and Dill Quiche 4
Salmon Orange and Arugula Salad 120
Salmon Pasta and Broccoli Salad 104
Salmon Pasta in Tomato Sauce 90
Salmon Pasta Salad with Yogurt-Herb Dressing 124
Salmon Roe and Greek Yogurt CanapE 142
Salmon Salad on Toast 156
Salmon Sandwich with Avocado and Egg 134
Salmon Sour Cream and Chives Sandwich 144
Salmon Spinach and Cottage Cheese Sandwich 136
Salmon Tikka Bites 74
Salmon with Caramelized Onion 82
Smoked Salmon and Cheese on Rye Bread 148
Smoked Salmon Omelet with Herbs 10
Smoked Salmon with Dill on Burger Bun 152
Soy Garlic Broiled Salmon 36
Soy Ginger Salmon 78
Spiced Roasted Salmon and Veggies 26
Spiced Salmon and Veggie Kebabs 58
Spicy Salmon with Honey-Ginger Glaze 34
Steamed Salmon with Lemon and Chives 62

T

Tabbouleh Salad with Salmon and Cucumber 106
Tuscan Salmon Pasta 92

Made in the USA
Las Vegas, NV
01 October 2023

78353747R10095